MORE WORDS OF PRAISE FOR *SAFE AS LIGHTNING*

"Scudder Parker writes musically with 'no irritable reaching' toward
quotidian beauty. With Buddha-like patience and attention toward such
immense particulars as the peonies, corms, and gladiolas in his garden,
he testifies to what he calls 'some shy part of me' [that] 'is always sitting…
in sun…on this cold porch…no wisdom, no plan; full of psalms, no notion
who I'm singing to.' In poem after poem, Parker divines by receiving, with
the result of apprehending the cosmos in the smallest things. 'The poem
of the world reveals itself / like a doe's hoof tapping ice till she can drink,'
he opines. Such lyrical perspicacity pervades his poems with true antinomies
that surprise and enlighten as personal revelations that resonate with gentle,
universal appeal."

> -Chard deNiord, Vermont Poet Laureate, 2015-2019

"Scudder Parker's poems have a Vermont flavor. He describes the world he
lives in and adds his personal philosophy. The poems allow us to see nature
in a different light and reflect on the meaning of life."

> -Governor Madeleine M. Kunin, author of
> *Coming of Age, My Journey to the Eighties*

"People who think of Scudder Parker as a former minister, Vermont
legislator, and political activist who, "by the way," writes poetry will have
to think again after reading his beautiful debut collection, *Safe as Lightning*.
This is the work of a poet who deserves the name, a poet of broad range
and deep sensibility. Among his many subjects and themes, one of the most
prominent is that of gratitude, 'a different eye that opens— / unnerving
in its great permissions.' It was certainly the emotion I felt after reading
his book."

> -Garret Keizer, author of *The World Pushes Back*

SAFE AS LIGHTNING

SAFE AS LIGHTNING

Poems by Scudder H. Parker

Scudder H. Parker (signature)

Rootstock Publishing

For permissions and author readings, contact the author at
https://www.scudderparker.net

Published by
Rootstock Publishing Poetry Series
Editor: Samantha Kolber
Montpelier, Vermont
www.rootstockpublishing.com

Book design by Mason Singer, Laughing Bear Associates.

Cover art by Adelaide Tyrol: "Balance-Bicknell's Thrush" [acrylic on wood panel, ©2009].
Interior illustrations by Adelaide Tyrol. Used with permission of the artist.

Library of Congress Control Number: 2020903375

ISBN-13: 978-1-57869-031-2
eISBN: 978-1-57869-034-3

Author photo by Susan M. Sussman.

These poems are dedicated to my grandchildren:
to everything and everyone they love now and
will learn to love; and to all who love them now
and will love them in the future:

Cashel, Gabriel, Sebastián, Ryan

ACKNOWLEDGMENTS

Some of the poems in this volume first appeared in the following publications:

Aquifer: The Florida Review Online: "Salvaging Beauty"
Crosswinds Poetry Journal: "The Poem of the World" and "Gratitude"
Eclectica: "Moose Bog" and "Lake Elmore"
La Presa: "Mississippi Kites"
Northern Woodlands Magazine: "Wild Turkeys"
Passager: "Our Turn" as "Love of Justice" and "My Mother's Art"
Ponder Review: "First Love," "Visitation," and "Rock Harvest"
Sky Island Journal: "Talent Show"
Stonecoast Review: "Safe as Lightning" and "Relinquished"
The Sun Magazine: "Davy Road" as "A Stranger Visits"
Twyckenham Notes: "Recognize," "Visit to Harpswell," "Sit Here,"
    "Humility," and "Tamarack"
Vermont Life Magazine: "The Saw," winner of the Ralph Nading Hill Prize
Wordrunner eChapbooks: "The Art of the Poem" as "Taken," and
    "Chamois Shirt"

Dear Reader,

I am pleased to share these poems with you. Please take your time with them.

There is nothing tidy about this volume.

Please feel encouraged to flip through, exploring as your interest takes you. I have not ordered by history, subject matter, literary form, or style. If there's an organizing principle it's the affection (or at least affinity) one poem seemed to feel for other poems.

Creating (or discovering) these poems has been a response to the invitation life keeps offering. I am astonished how much stays unsaid. Most of it doesn't need to; some of it absolutely shouldn't. Of course, I don't presume to say for you what only you can say, but poetry does feel like a way I get to share what I hope you will find familiar, or at least in some measure, recognizable, experience.

Our family moved to North Danville, Vermont, when I was nine years old. My sister and two brothers came to Vermont in that move. My youngest brother was the first "native" Vermonter in the family. We started dairy farming steeped in ignorance. We loved the land but did not thrive as farmers. After our main farmhouse burned, my father became a minister, but we continued to own the land, growing Christmas trees to keep the "home farm" productive.

I was a Protestant minister for over 20 years and a Vermont State Senator for four terms. In 2006, I ran for Governor of Vermont. I am a longtime activist and organizer (anti-war, community housing, food security, recycling). After working in state government on energy issues for 13 years, I was a policy consultant in energy efficiency, renewable energy, and utility policy for the decade prior to my retirement.

While I have enjoyed each professional role I have been in, I hope the poems won't feel too shaped by any of them, but instead, act as a way of sharing some of what has touched and tugged at me over the years.

Sincerely,

Scudder H. Parker

Scudder H. Parker

TABLE OF CONTENTS

I want to extend my special thanks to Adelaide Tyrol who generously provided the cover painting, and the interior drawings which appeared in the wonderful publication Northern Woodlands Magazine. *Her gift of sight and her stunning imagination should inform how we all learn to see the world around us.*

reveals itself
like a doe's hoof tapping ice
till she can drink.

Startles like the rust of purple on this fall's
forsythia leaves, though it may have used that small voice
every year, unheard.

Blinks like red and blue potatoes,
dug this morning, drying in the sun, testing
their startled untrained eyes.

It's the unexpected tickle, the fit of shared
laughter in our urgency of touching that becomes
another way of making love. It's an ocean

beach of pebbles that suddenly
starts singing, each stone its own tink;
together, a glorious indifferent song.

And it's the voice of each bird I have only heard
as morning chorus landing with its own song
and bright perfect body in my brain.

It is even—now I begin to see them—the subtraction
of birds, taking summer with them, too busy
to announce their leaving.

The poem of the world wants me to wake
in my own body; it is astonished I might let
these supple bones grow brittle.

It is the sudden thing I trust.

A man in clothes the shape of sleep
pushes his battered bicycle,
wire baskets front and back,
halfway up the drive and stops.

He watches me raking gravel.
"You live here now?" I pause,
lean on my rake. "I'm trying."
We gossip like old neighbors.

His family logged pine and maple.
A few cows and chickens. Some summers
a bear got all the corn. I tell him
a bear got ours last summer.

The house and barn were "down there,
where you have your woodpile now.
The house was small and cold as hell.
The barn was built better."

We go down, explore lilac,
sprawling roses, honeysuckle,
clumps of double daffodils,
stacked granite slabs that held the barn.

No sign of the house foundation.
Five generations in this place,
and I, three years.

Twice since then I've seen him,
picking up empties. Once,
just his bike, leaning against a tree.

ROCK HARVEST

When I'm digging potatoes
and the fork hits rock, I dig for rock.
The logic of it seems clear to me.
                                    Susan,
whom I have accused of conducting
"non-linear conversations,"
leans back on her gloved hands
and smiles.

There are clutches of bold reds,
blues camouflaged against dark loam,
gold and pink Augusta—this winter's
nourishment.
                    But I am seized
by grey subsoil, rust-streaked, dense
with shattered rocks, some rounded granite
nestled with them.

When I clank and probe
to test a boulder's residence,
Susan says it's time for her to go pick
winter squash.
                    "Good idea" I say as I reach
for iron bar and shovel.
Some work becomes
its own insistence.

That's how farmers built walls that weave across our hills.
Every year a new stone crop nudges sunward,
quiet, but determined.
                            Above ground
they grow beards of moss
and lichen, give shelter
to small creatures.

These are fields you can finally plow without stopping
every twenty feet to curse, with walls that never keep
a creature out.
                    Next summer, the soil will be

a little deeper. Twenty years
from now, someone else
may garden here.

I pause, watch Susan gather squash.
She has already picked up the potatoes;
it's her way of being gracious.
                              We both know
what it is to dig and worry at a stubbornness
the mind takes hold of that calls out
to be dislodged.

MISSISSIPPI KITES
(Lower Rio Grande Valley)

An undulating, seething swarm
tugs against its own elastic boundary
in the distance of the clouds.
It's small enough to burn my hand
if I could reach it, but before I can,
it blinks into the whiteness of the sky.

      "Probably kites," says a friend,
      "raptors in their migrating dance."
      I only know the slow roil of kettles
      over Mt. Philo; hawks assembled but
      alone, gyring up, then pouring out,
      in their deliberate southern flow.

Last light in McAllen, Texas. We search
for green parakeets—but kites! Kites!
erupt from a different dimension;
fifties, hundreds, thousands, take
the city; the populace, heads down,
oblivious to the vast convention.

      Here is that great mass—a live dot
      journeying the sky—unleashed. They sweep in,
      swarm the suburbs, then suddenly deflate,
      dissolve into the manicured remaining trees—
      invisible again, returned to rest
      in part of their diminishing estate.

A fever of kites ghosts my sleep,
shivers my body with its wild invitation.
Next morning at Frontera, where fifteen
acres of unmanaged thicket have been
saved by Audubon, an elegant grey bird
turns, stares at us, lifts up, resumes its flight.

TAMARACK

Suddenly I see it, standing autumn gold, small
in a small wet field between an old barn
and houses marching uphill out of town.

It has sprouted, rooted, grown, at home
in marshy ground. It could be joined by alder,
red maple, rising through tall, temporary grass.

It's like my grade-school classmate, living
his separate life in our North Danville neighborhood:
we made friends slowly but, it seemed, for good.

Soft green spring tufts, wild purple cones,
even this gold—dry and dropped by winter—
and his uncalculating kindness, gone.

I doubt the tamarack, preoccupied
with season-toil, attends to my attention,
but I, for my long blindness, feel disloyal.

I wasn't trained this way; I say I never chose
that quick tinge of scorn for those who
struggle on, unaware they've been forsaken.

THE VOICE HE GREW UP WITH

Increasingly the names of things
fall off like tired labels from manila folders,
lodge at the bottom of file drawers
or float around the room like butterflies.
This leads to lengthy explanations,
difficult to follow: "You know, that movie
where the guy who was in this other movie…"
I feel a new kinship with my mother.

At a dinner with friends, everyone else
is full of food and conversation. I sit
in awe of the painting—a sapling
in a clearing—aching with its solitude.
Suddenly they look at me. A question
has been asked; I've been turned to for opinion.
My mother's helpful whisper offers:
"Tell them the quiche is delicious."

She lives in a landscape without courtesy.
It's not a terrifying place for her.
She knows her husband's voice is gone.
                                        Her
grandson visits, talks about summers at the farm,
how they stayed with him through all his wars.
She has not spoken in weeks.
As he walks out the door she says "thank you"
in the voice he grew up with.

CONVERSION

1.

Our second spring in Hardwick
I was sixteen and hopelessly lusting
after Jackie LeCours. I wasn't supposed
to fall in love with a Catholic
because they'd make you raise
your children for the pope,
my father said.

So, when I offered, half joking, but
full of hope, to give back her pictures
if she paid for each one with a kiss,
and she said "yes" without hesitating,
I panicked and sent them to her in the mail.

Every Sunday, my father stood
in the confidence of his black robe
pouring the unction of his words
over the congregation. I watched from
the choir faces like familiar rocks
along a shore, half waiting for,
half submitting to, the tide.

His determined giving had begun
three years before, after the last child was born,
and he became a preacher like his father.
Steadily, God mushroomed in our family,
finally moving in like a determined aunt
who used to visit only occasionally,
but now had come to set things right.

2.

It was a weekend in that second spring.
I was in the house alone. I woke
on Saturday, my senses quickened;
my heart stunned by patience.
A sweet taste haunted my mouth,
fed me like no food I could remember.

Suddenly I was at home here.

My mind filled with promises; my hands
were restless to bless.

It was knowledge, not insistence.
It stayed with me for days.

Because I had no name for it
I used my father's word for love,
and dressed it in an old coat called conversion.

3.

I don't remember the pictures clearly,
or how I got them. Black and white
snapshots of girls I knew, clowning
at a slumber party. Jackie stopped me
in the hall at school, standing close
to thank me for them. She smiled
and said she wanted to be friends.

Suddenly there was less danger;
the taste of her lips, the shape
of her breasts, went with her as she left.

I began to realize I could survive
under cover of goodness. I felt
the holy promiscuity of saints—
a yielding, terrible and all-consuming,
that sometimes is delight
and sometimes
its own subtle form of flight.
That summer she went out with Ernie LeMay.

It seemed like power to take my fear
and turn it into kindness.
They seemed to love me for it. It felt pure,
and I needed something pure.
I never thought of it as sacrifice.

And for the first time I could taste
the metallic residue of longing.

COMFORTER

1.

Across Route 100 from the yellow barn
and outbuildings that were once
the dairy farm for the state psychiatric hospital,
a cedar hedge guards Waterbury's graveyard.

I ask you to stop the car. It's midwinter,
but I imagine a cluster of family,
and, separated by the open grave,
the one who by profession offers comfort.

It's the moment after the last words have been said.
The men who wait at a distance,
leaning against the pickup truck,
smoking cigarettes, shift at this pause,
watch the living ebb away.

Their long-handled shovels
can begin their work.
I watch as they have watched,
from my own distance.

> Every time, I hoped the loveliness
> of grief might heal me, the sudden tumult
> of children's tears, old men crying
> with the ungainliness of buildings coming
> down.

> I held the fine tool of the ceremony
> in my hands, asking without asking,
> They left me with silence
> when they took their lives back home.

2.

I remember the summer when this farm
was still making milk for the hospital,
thick cream for coffee, and work
for the inmates. I was an intern
anxious to help the unfortunate.

What I learned was how to change
bedclothes for the dying, to clean excrement
gently from the folds of uncherished flesh.

One night on the admissions ward,
I held a glass of water toward a man
with eyes too wild to ever see me.

I learned to be almost good enough to quiet
those wild eyes, to help the hand
reach from its darkness toward the glass.

And I learned the quiet treachery
of such determined goodness,
how it can only think of leaving
when it believes its work is done.

>Yesterday a streak of winter sun
>crept across our bed. I lay down
>in that sun and called to you; from somewhere
>you came and touched me.

TODAY

This morning a ladybug
appears from nowhere.
It circumnavigates my breakfast plate.

The cat eyes finches through the glass
who arrive to feed on black oil
sunflower seed from Kansas.

I used to understand so many things.
Now everything surprises me;
anger shows up on my doorstep

like an orphan.
Sadness is a thread of light
I try to pick off the carpet.

There is nothing
I am qualified to rescue.
I am learning to be patient.

AVALON, NEW JERSEY

Gulls are watching everything.
Loons bob in the harbor. Human
dreams are lured to assemble here
in houses no one lives in
eight months of the year.

Block after block, they nudge
up to the line of fickle dunes.
We visit on a raw March day.
Each empty street has its own
stairway to the sand and sea.

Only builders—hired to complete
the dreams—park their trucks,
crack locked-up winter doors,
install a porch, new cabinets,
gather to gossip in the street.

The new seawall, built with
boulders bigger than refrigerators
from some dismantled mountain
guards the north. The sand keeps drifting
south, composing its own new land.

One boulder is a marbled slab
of granite; pink, white, veins
of black. It seems astonishingly pure.
If this were Arthur's Avalon,
this is the rock that held Excalibur.

No gardens here, though legend says
in that other Avalon—the one
unbuilt, unfound—apples flourish,
grains and grape vines grow almost
untended in the fertile ground.

A COAL PLANT IN IOWA

that never got built
provides me with stacks of paper for the printer.
And I have scribbled notes, made lists for years
on backsides of evidence from earnest witnesses
declaring benefits from burning coal.

The first drafts of this poem were
all printed on the other side of a
"2007 long-term reliability assessment."

How quickly the enormity
of what did not happen eludes me.

It was January; the wind roared snow
across the fields of Marshalltown.
Most recited that the billion-dollar
plant would make things better.
I was there to disagree.

They still package beef in Marshalltown,
and now that same wind makes its own electricity.

It was a ritual of formal testimony
to "establish need."
There were rules to guide what could be said.
I dressed appropriately;
spoke my careful argument.

There are rules for poetry as well, but
it is easier to break them.

That other talk goes on and on—
the words and rules so slow to change.

At least one coal plant doesn't.
A foot-high stack of paper
waiting blank side up
is all that's left of it.

UNPREPARED

My brother and his partner always called us
together—Thanksgiving, Christmas, Easter
were the excuses. "Bring creamed onions, latkes,
that green bean casserole, brussels sprouts Peter
won't eat." My brother in his late life reverence
offered blessings we all could pause and welcome.

How delicate those gatherings of celebration!
Why did we think them ordinary at the time?
Each meal an invention; scraps of families,
strangers; conversations bouncing over ruts like
laughter. And Alan, cheerful with a lovely mess,
thrilled by such unofficial holiness.

When the freshet in his brain washed him away,
it was the shock of a winter flood. Snowmelt to our waists;
breath shriveled in our throats; stove hissed, shattered.
Unprepared (as we always are) we were even
denied time to assemble the stick huts of pretense,
recite the rituals that stand in for confidence.

I brought the tiller one month later; steel tines
raked garden soil again in preparation. I harangued
submerged boulders from the footprint of a barn.
My brother's partner, her son, and I heaved
some to the streambank. The tiller began leaking oil.
She said she could work around the others.

Two and a half years later we share tea
and a frittata as the cold stream fills and leaves
the pond beside the house. She says, "I miss his body,
his humor—not his way with money!" Then the tears.
"What's hardest is the fear I'll never again find
companionship with such a passionate mind."

NO DOUBT

The year's great confidence of leaves is spent.
And we, so busy losing, count it loss—
all absence equally seems permanent.

Our snowshoes on the snowcrust leave no dent.
Beech leaves cling and shiver like pale ghosts;
they, and our loved ones' days, are fully spent.

We're resurrection-schooled. The brave intent
is comfort: "The thaw will follow on the frost;
lovers return; the seasons? Permanent."

Yet so many quit and seem not to (or can't) repent
their leaving—parents, species, stars, cross
to the calm void. Another voice dissents

in counterpoint, reminding we are meant
to live like hummingbirds as they accost
their blooms, essential and impermanent.

It's spring. I am in loss. This is my present:
to be in love with everything, and more
with lovely things that will be quickly spent;
still more, because the loss is permanent.

FIRST LOVE
(for John)

1.

You and I were busy, fifty years ago
exploring our ways to love. The road
we take today over Stannard Mountain
used to be unplowed in winter, and, like love,
an adventure in any season. Its metaphor
was different for my father. Since it was

> the shortest route between two places
> where our family lived, it stood for good
> sense and valor in the face of danger—
> the danger he acknowledged. We drive it
> this late September day of our renewing
> friendship, creep along, slow to find our way.

Fall colors are still muted, not yet
at peak. Today's road is "improved,"
as Vermonters say. But we know how
a few years of neglect could leave it gullied
and impassable. We have both seen small
victories won, then rapidly undone.

2.

Spring of our junior year, we drove
from Hardwick to our bereft North Danville
farm. The house had burned; the cows were gone.
But this was our great adventure in your father's
Model A. We came the long way (Route 15,
through Danville) to stay in the surviving cottage.

> The dirt road to North Danville Village
> was a sea of ruts that spring (and every spring).
> The high narrow wheels rode through like Jesus
> walking on the water. We said we could conquer
> anything. We lit a fire, hiked, cooked meals,
> companioned in the sagging double bed.

Your gentle investigation of my body
sweetened me; was the first time I let myself
feel cherished. You touched the moles,
the curves, the prairies of my skin.
This, I thought, was what friendship could be;
but I pulled back when you wanted me.

3.

That summer I fell in love with Kathy Hancock,
her music, mind, and slender body.
My parents asked why you and I spent
less time together. "I think he's a little
jealous of Kathy." Blank looks, surprise,
then panic erupted behind their eyes.

> At least they didn't punish us, but fear
> took over. That courage my father honored
> paused, stepped back, turned remote and formal.
> They took their fear to a psychiatrist,
> warned the other children, sought comfort
> in some confidence that I was *normal.*

I ask if you remember when we hit 100
on the road to Woodbury just out of town.
Your father owned the Ford dealership;
you always had a car to get around.
"I don't remember that specific day,
but I drove fast a lot, mostly alone," you say.

4.

The valley opens before us. So much color
waits in this Northeast Kingdom! Burke Mountain
already hinting at November purple. I say
"I'm sorry I didn't love you the same way."
You pause, "I'm just glad to have my friend
again." We let our sadness fill the car.

> You say you were thirty-four and still
> pretending. Then you set yourself free.

Your mother decided she would teach your
first lover to cook your favorite casserole.
She thought that he was good for you.
As mothers do, she always sort of knew.

You just keep driving slower. Cars pull up,
honk, swing out to pass. I imagine them
muttering "Old leaf peepers!" Even with affection
and good intent we let fifty years of silence
flow between us. That's how the injury
prevails. Decades harden like cement.

5.

As we drive, we find our way to talk.
You ask about my sister, what it feels like
growing old. It seems as though our families
pile into the back seat, desperate
to share with us, each other, full of their
own stories, some familiar, most untold.

    You want to see the farm. My mother
    and stepfather died last summer. The cottage
    where we slept has returned to emptiness.
    My brother greets us; his good friend,
    Tom, is turning an old maple (one of those
    that line the road) to chunks of firewood.

His blue battered tractor's bucket is near full.
You say, "Ford...good choice." I joke that you might
try to sell a new one. "No way," says Tom,
"This here is my last tractor!" You say,
"The new ones are great." It feels like we could
pause here, past in present, talk all day.

    We drive to Peacham, where my grandfather
    and his second wife (who left her partner, Marian,
    to take up her new life) are buried up among
    the massive pines. We get out. You call me as we search
    the lichened stones. You say what I am thinking:
    "Another thing it's better not to do alone."

ART OF THE POEM

I imagine myself a cook, and someone
has been stealing my poems again;
I just left fresh ones on the windowsill to cool.
Before I could get back...gone!

Sometimes I'm desperate and when
the nephew of a Nigerian prince
urgently needs a small poetry deposit
to secure a vulnerable fortune, I respond at once.

Generally, I just leave them on the counter
hoping the children and grandchildren
will find them tempting and grab
a few in passing, like blueberries.

I haunt my wife; latest edits in hand,
embarrassed by my urgency. I want her
to want to steal these words I have not yet
found the way to use in conversation.

EARLY MEMORIES OF JESUS

1.

Remember how we wished
(before we became embarrassed
by the wish) that our parents—
released from their bruising clumsiness—
would search harder for the words
to tell their wonder in us,
noticing every detail, touching
our hair, our cheeks, making
brilliant guesses, their hearts
breaking open with our flight?

How could they spend so much time
backstage getting ready,
twisting sweaty palms together,
rehearsing someone else's wisdom
as we slipped away from them?

Year after year the boulders
grew unmentioned in the kitchen,
a kind of eternity accumulating in them.

2.

Despite my parents' confidence
in God's good intentions,
I never believed that Jesus
was overcome by charity
when he relinquished that inheritance
where the sheep stay forever painted on the hills.

I suspected he couldn't wait to get away.
After eons of wheedling,
he finally got to God by calling it a sacrifice;
and God, who suspected what was really happening
and knew that he had failed,
pressed some folding money in his hand
as he was leaving.

3.

Though I never spoke his name,
he was the friend who daydreamed with me
through all the early lectures
and woke up for the field trips,
thrilled if the teacher's shoes got muddy.
He could find wild ginger
under leaves bleached and frailed by winter;
blue cohosh uncurling fingers
the color of evening in a maple woods.
We found and ate wild onions, green flags,
red bulbs flecked with loam,
so spring would infect our breath.

When we heard my father calling,
he urged me to keep to the wildness of our hiding places:
the cave under spruce boughs
arching down to moss in the high pasture;
a bracken forest, where, a foot above our heads,
sun collected like honey
and dripped down to us.

His vigilance was wonderful.
Whenever he felt the dark shapes of caution
clumping in me, he tackled
and wrestled me to earth,
wild with impatience.
He held me struggling
until my stomach cramped with laughter.

Again and again
we tried the loudness of our voices,
and listened for them
coming back to us across the valley.

4.

He never talked about the Crucifixion
and I never asked.
It seemed to be someone else's story,

something the people wanted
and the reporters put together.
The details couldn't have come from him;
it was as though the promises he had to make to get away
finally caught up with him.

Without the story, he was invisible,
no safer or less safe than any of us,
just another bright but troubled child.

5.

Now we are both older;
I try to stay in touch with him
and see as much around me as I can.
He has a small place on the edge of town.
I visited the other day.
We walked together in the woods.
He said there is more light from the east
since they cut the virgin hemlock stand
and used the clearing to stockpile gravel.
They were rebuilding the highway,
to make it straight and wide.

We pulled wild onions
to add to our supper soup.
Each year, he said, the night sky lightens
from another building
and the stars retreat a little,
even though the field of balsam where he lives
is on its way back to forest
and has grown beyond the threat of Christmases.

I asked if he had heard from God.
He said he hadn't
and still missed him,
but he understood
how easy it is to get preoccupied.

As we talked, the moon—
the somewhat predictable

temporary moon—that tugs
twice every day at our bodies
rose like a fragile egg
in the denim sky.

SAFE AS LIGHTNING

Long before guilt was invented
this stream managed rocks without it—

never a threat or wheedle—just shifted them
when strength was gathered. Changes

from every storm were there for my
exploration. That's how its small

riffles and dark pools became
such freedom for me. Neither worms

I pierced, nor speckled fish I hooked
cried out in accusation. In turn

they claimed me, taught me to fin in place
beneath a dark green overhang of rock.

Oh! How the heart is taught to bargain;
search the hard ground of obedience

and its deceptions. I would rather
sink my feet in black loamy banks

where a holy beaver pond spills its
disconcerting welcome through the trees.

There is no promise I will be safe
if I relinquish. It is a place where

for a few years brook trout fatten
and the silt accumulates, until

some torrent tears the sticks apart and I
come exploring next June's fertile mud.

Nothing I can promise spares
the children. My grandson shudders

at colliding arguments of thunder
but will not be denied the lightning.

BESIDE THE GARDEN

A mound of laden edamame plants
sits beside me on the soft
September lawn; shade and light
are strewn around. My old
red-handled clipper snipped them,
left their rich roots in the ground.

I like the clean click of steel
against the flat brass anvil.
Armful by armful I bring them here,
select the right arrangement
in the sun, sit down, tug pods off
till their generosity is mine.

Could this be what
heaven promises? But who
could replicate it somewhere
else? They'd never get it right.
Monarch on yellow zinnias;
the sun stealing into night.

I have this perfect broken gift,
and sadness, its companion.
I leave the empty stalks,
take inside the fuzzy beans,
boil them, pinch them open,
taste ecstatic pearls of green.

VISITATION

Perhaps it was our carpet,
the color of vast deserts,
that lured the black beetle
with elegant orange Fabergé
designs. For all I know
it teleported from Tunisia
or the early thirteenth century.
It stayed for days.

Wherever it was from,
whatever time, I'm certain
in the universe of beetles
it was no extraordinary thing to do.
It was my noticing,
the surprise of its beauty,
my urge to have it stay,
that made it a visitation.

Its calm precision, the orange
on such perfect black. The cats
showed studious respect.
I don't know where it went,
but there are tiny fractures
in the rules that shape me.
I think I became more patient;
there was no promise of return.

CHRISTMAS TREE

My Jewish wife, partly in jest, insists
on Christmas trees. That quiet smile:
"Isn't this one of the benefits I get
from taking up with a gentile?"

Resistance is both foolish and futile:
my brother grows trees for a living;
I was a preacher twenty years; she is,
of all of us, most talented in giving.

Evergreen—solstice custom, deftly
stolen from Europe's pagan tribes.
The priests knew a living sign is power
when the searching heart subscribes.

Our tree's on a closed porch; we ornament,
thread looped on twig: painted egg, green
toy canoe, loon with a broken beak,
collected, protected, for years. At night

just tiny lights, but all still there:
grandson-hung green & yellow God's eye
his mother made, bright wire basket
woven in Vietnam, birds poised to fly,

tiny silver flute, straw Star of David.
An assembly of tokens that persists
long after we've accepted and forgotten
more decorated and impressive gifts.

The porch is cold; the tree slow to shed.
We wait some weeks; daylight grows stronger.
Tree, ornaments, still in our winter lives,
welcome as good friends to stay longer.

Yet something in us finally says, "Enough."
We tissue-wrap the ornaments, hide
them gently in our drawer of days; restore
the tree to its simplicity outside.

In drifts by the bird feeder out front,
a friendly avian resting place;
patient pagan again, as we
conduct our changeling faiths.

BORROWED EARTH
(The Turf Farm near Zapata)

Golden Plovers alight here at will. We
who would see them, stop to ask permission.
Piles of pipe, blue plastic resting like
collapsed veins in the ditches;
huge wheels poised to roll across the land.
The vast machinery of water
dispenses life at its convenience.

And where the water is, the green
of foreign grass. Plovers feed
where a ground-knife has freed sod
for incarnation on some upstart lawn.
They come for the incidental meal,
scenting another mysterious
appearance of the Rio Grande.

We drive the lane that alternates powder
and mud. Birds strut, pause, probe the ground.
And here:
         a sudden fragile garden grows:
corn, chard, tomatoes, bathed in dust, just
a few feet wide.
           We won't be here
this evening when workers come to coax,
water, tend this borrowed bit of earth.

STARR COUNTY PARK, TEXAS

His skin is like desert varnish, dark
from dust and time and sun.
He has laid claim to the rotting
gazebo, its array of faded
novels, unused self-help books.
It's ninety degrees and just getting
started, so we join him in the shade.

Someone still mows the field.
The camp sites offer cracked cement tables,
tilted brick benches. He is gracious,
we are awkward in what has become
his personal public space. He used
to work for Pepsi, making labels,
until he couldn't take it any longer.
Now he says, he's "on his journey."

So are we. He shows his "snake stick"
with two pencil points to hold his catch.
Snake hunting has been hard the last
few days. We are on the prowl for
vermillion flycatchers, binoculars
at the ready. He says, "They're all over
the place, singing in the morning."

Time for lunch; we get full bags
and coolers from the van. He readies his
moldy bread and milk. We offer cheese
and turkey in a spinach wrap, water
in a plastic bottle…then grapes and a
couple oranges. He says, "Thank you very
kindly. You should look down by my camp."

It's the only site occupied. Hammock,
ancient cookstove, small bags of belongings,
strangely welcoming. We find the bird,
its tiny, insistent brilliance. A creature
just surviving, brings us pride, delight,
fulfillment. He knew it would. We watch it whisk
from tree to tree; then go back up to thank him.

PRESENT

In the photograph on our bedroom wall
I walk behind Mollie, our first Jersey cow,
up a pasture flecked with dandelions.
Solemn, stick in hand, I gaze down.
She looks calmly past the picture's
frame to her spring-fed pasture pool.

> A corridor of trees divides this field
> from fields beyond. The brook that finds
> shade there rises from the root-nest
> of an elm, umbrella-arching on the left.
> I can hear the language of that water,
> not pristine, but delicate and clear.

Leaves are barely forming on the trees;
a grove of poplars, first to colonize
the open land, sits to the right; spruce, pruned
dense by itching cows, are cones of black.
The forest yielded this land grudgingly
for farming: "Use it, or we'll take it back."

> At the time it all seemed permanent.
> I was ten. We had moved up from the city,
> ambitious to be farmers, learning
> honest work. We milked the cows by hand.
> The photographer could glimpse a story
> we were living but didn't understand.

I worked on all the land we owned.
My farm brother does it still. Flowers
and grasses thin as tree-shade deepens.
The woods have claimed most fields since then.
The brook still rises, runs its finger
through the valley, irrepressible and plain.

I don't know where the meteorite is now—
round nubbled rock, flattened like a meadow
muffin, iron-heavy. It has resumed
its ancient status as unowned.

Fifty years ago, we brought it home—
our strange catch from an afternoon fishing
Houghton Brook. Resting in clear water
we marveled it had hurtled through our air.

A rusted pump and handle sprouted
from the brook bed too; iron wheel rims leaned
against stone walls—elements the same,
but different—both had been human-tamed.

The trout swam over it oblivious.
It could have come eons ago, seared
its way through a mile of ice—or found
this pool last year—still ageless, wonderful.

At the museum in town, the curator
just laughed and gave no answer, did not trust
our story (so common when the galaxy
delivers us its weighty cosmic dust.)

I haven't searched for it. I don't want it
rusting in the shed, shelved in that museum,
or hammered on some anvil. Like other things,
it is at home, lost, in North Danville.

WHAT WE LEARNED

"Shitkickers" was the name used for barn boots
we wore to grade school in North Danville.
We compared with pride, having kicked a fair amount
early each morning doing chores—pitching hay,
feeding cows, milking, shoveling out the gutter.

But when we got to high school, freshman year,
the name was used for us—the scent they couldn't bear.
We learned to smell it on ourselves.
It became a word we used against each other,
wielding it without instruction.

All those years of training to be patriots;
hiding from bombs beneath our desks, fed frozen
peas, tuna from conquered seas, soft bread from our plains.
Glib claims of greatness in the air. Our differences
dangerous as weapons, waiting everywhere.

BODY OF WORK

1.

A day with a good taste hidden in it
that your mouth keeps finding
hour after hour—I remember
them from childhood,
like the opening of partridge season
when I could stalk
yellow-leaved apple trees
after school, poised
for the sweet *thrummm*
of mottled birds exploding at my feet.
Even our teacher grew lovely
with the advancing afternoon.
The shotgun was waiting
to cradle in my arm; I
could feel its blue metal,
smell the oil on my hand.

This morning, thirty-five
years later, I took the
blade from my Troy-Bilt
chipper to the man
with a plywood saw blade outside
his shop announcing
he could sharpen anything.
He took the nicked steel,
asked, "Just one?" and
clamped it on his almost
new machine. After he finished
his Styrofoam cup of coffee
and pronounced opinions about unions,
Bush, Clinton and Leahy,
he gave it back to me, gleaming,
ready to cut. All day at the office
I felt the satisfaction of it.

2.

How strange to feel the world is good
because a well-sharpened tool
waits for you in the car.
I remember, as I stood there
watching the grinder
find the fire hidden in the steel
(the way the blade would later
find the wood-sparks
in the limbs we fed it) thinking:
*This is the world men lived in
in my childhood.*
An old circular saw blade
rested on a piece of 2 x 4,
with a chronicle of file nicks
in the gaps between its teeth.
I remembered Hubert Simons
and the "saw rig" he had made
from a Model T.

One fall, we cut eight cords
of firewood in a day.
I brought the log lengths;
my father held them on the tray
and cut them like green beans
against the living blade. Hubert caught
and threw the stove-sized chunks
until the truck bed filled.
Night after night in my sleep,
I could hear the blade's scream,
the whine and groan
of the engine in its rhythm
through the wood. I felt
again how I sat heavy with work,
unable to tell the difference
between satisfaction and exhaustion,
my mind empty with gloating,
my hands resting in work's shape.

3.

A week passes before I put the blade
back on the chipper.
It waits, wrapped in an old T-shirt
on the pantry shelf.
I make it a ritual, greasing each bolt
and nut, spraying the surfaces with oil.
I start the almost wholly
unnecessary machine
which purrs through spruce limbs
and frost-darkened refuse
from the garden, preparing a huge nest
of compost to teem all winter
with the memory of summer.
It is what might be called work.
I remember how it is to forget my body
in the rush of what must be done.
I'll do it over in my sleep
and come out to admire things tomorrow.

Hubert always grew solemn with
delight; my father pressed
the point of his tongue against
his upper lip. They talked to each other
like boys conspiring.
When something needed tinkering,
as it always did, I was sent
for the nine-inch crescent,
or the steel-handled screwdriver
as their heads bent together
arguing solutions. No matter

how serious they were, I knew it was subversion
by the ones who made the rules.
It was like sugaring, sweet freedom
in disguise, a work they invented
in the middle of the work they had to do.
I brought them the tools they needed.
We got things running
and in time the job was done.

BLESSING

You compose a table
from all the tables in the house,
drape it with old linen till it snakes
through living and dining rooms
like a Chinese dragon.

White metal lawn chairs come up
from basement slumber,
antiques from the bedroom,
where a week of clothes lands on the floor.

You dig to the back of the drawer
for cheap stainless, then the family silver;
untie ribbons hugging it in chamois cloth.

Wine glasses, from pewter to crystal,
alternate around the table,
suggesting a symmetry in their history.

You remember the spoons
that melted in the fire
no one here remembers,
and the fourth and missing crystal glass.

Guests bring the cold air in,
each with their offering of food.
Laughter and greeting for your friends,
who embrace all guests, familiar and just met,
because you love them all.

Voices rise in the living room over wine,
crackers, chopped liver, baba ghanoush.
There's that last-minute rush, the comfort of it—
this in, this out, of oven or refrigerator.

It's as you bring your kugel to the table
the absence races through you; the laughter here
invites the laughter that is gone.
How can we be joyful in the company of loss?

Your knees are weak, you lean into your closest friend;
pause, slowly start to breathe. And we begin,
now that the meal is blessed.

WHEN WE GROW OUR OWN

I park in Montpelier with a cubic yard of compost
in the truck. I'm on my way home to plant garlic.
"Treasure" I think and carefully lock
the doors. Of course, the black gold lies exposed,
ready to be scooped by covetous hands
into ready canvas shopping bags.

It will be even more precious, I imagine,
when strawberries stop arriving in clear plastic
from Mexico and families there begin to grow
the food they long for. Could young and old,
living in cardboard in California, soon
find fresh vegetables daily at their feet?

Families will parade around our town
with towers of brussels sprouts. Red wagons
will be piled with carrots and cabbages.
Neighbors will stop to explain about celeriac;
brag they're growing sweet corn June to October;
observe that blueberries are taking over.

Food scraps from Sarducci's, horse manure,
last autumn's leaves, all ready to work again.
Think what it might lead to! My friend,
who lectures me about "economy of labor,"
will beg compost, a mug of leek and potato soup,
a blue Hubbard squash for his neighbor.

ON YESTERDAY'S RIVER

I'm still dazzled by yesterday's river;
sunlight patient, stroking sly, elusive water;
eagle soaring downstream, claiming everything.

We thought we had a plan, but what did we know?
That was the joy of it—graveled shallows; deep
current tugging kayaks through willow screens.

The railroad tries to river-manage with massive
granite rubble—blocks that seem resolute
until the full flood tumbles them.

All my life I've driven beside this river,
crossed it on bridge after crumbling bridge.
But there we were, captured, and we knew it.

Yesterday's shoes sit here, soaked with time.
How the bedrock swam upstream, whale-sleek,
staring at us with its small quartz eye.

MY AFFECTION FOR TOADS

I find myself talking to them
initially as though they were
small children, then correct, trying
to be respectful, adult to adult.

Even then I am too enthusiastic,
as though greeting someone I was
certain I must know on Main Street,
who stares back, struggling to recognize.

About the tiller and its bad
behavior I apologize, though
remarkably, that relative made it
to tall grass with only a small limp.

No courtesy, no cleverness or deft
protection; only this odd elegance,
tripping, rolling over, revealing its
creamy underside in August peonies.

TALENT SHOW

She played trumpet
at a talent show in the church basement
badly, with enormous enthusiasm.
We snickered with almost no
restraint at the music and her
enormous, heaving, eighth grade breasts.

Fragments like this
come flying at me
like deadly pieces of space litter,
still in orbit after all these years;
and here I am in the small safety
of my delicate identity capsule.

She may be a grandmother by now.
We might recognize each other
in the checkout line at Shaw's.
She'd ask in her husky voice
about my sister and brothers.
I'd tell her the usual something.

Perhaps I could wait for her
to go through the line, walk with her
to the parking lot, ask about her life
and listen. I've learned to do that.
I suspect she'd forgive easily,
if I had the courage to ask.

Or, she might barely remember.
For her it was just another bunch
of stupid boys acting like they did.
Probably much worse happened, yet
here she is, listening to an old man
explain what she's long understood.

SIT HERE

A fine cable runs from peony petal
to light fixture above the kitchen table.
A spider smaller than a dewdrop
drew it from herself. In her ascending dance
she's indifferent with assurance.

I bring in blowsy boisterous blooms
knowing I bring the family too. Small ants
scoot toward breadcrumbs on the cutting board.
They and six earwigs swiftly set up shop;
I quarrel only fitfully with them to stop.

Creatures emerge for days; buds surge
open, shoulder into one another;
occupants visit bloom to bloom—
yellow spider quits the yellow peony,
glows in a new magenta petal home.

Two days—one blossom or another
tires, drops deep coral petals as though
a child released them in oncoming sleep.
Drifts pile on table, slip to chair, still more
colors, tarnished, spill across the floor.

Sunlight fills the kitchen but keeps moving.
Nothing stops; everything slows. Beauty
slips away from nouns and adjectives, the vase,
the sturdy shelf. It takes all my courage
just to sit here with my less impatient self.

WE NEVER KNOW

The small racket was a wren's song
in the brush beside the garden.
I heard new notes; looked but couldn't find.
Today it hops up on the railing,
its small body perches in my mind.

That's our spring—purple finch, indigo
bunting, distant thrush—brief greetings.
Sometimes they come, sometimes not here.
How I want "always" for the hummingbird and us. But I'm learning...I don't dare.

WILD TURKEYS
(East St. Johnsbury, 1989)

They are in parts of this state
already, though not many

in this northern kingdom
where spruce and fir begin,

where oak is scarce and ironwood,
an occasional orphan left by loggers.

You can't chase them; they only come
to patience and to calling.

It's not just an apology to their plump
hypnotized cousins, this invitation;

but a sacrament
for what they've never lost.

I want a forest full of twenty-pound spirits;
I am calling with twenty-nine oak trees,

the grooming of beech, young groves
of lace-twigged ironwood,

pasture apples pruned
and released.

One day I will find a feather
at field's edge; I will hear

their gabble in the woods;
a dark shape will glide across a logging road,

or appear in a December dawn,
digging for winter apples.

ELMS

All the way from Pittsburgh to Phoenix
the men behind us talked marketing
and never once gave a clue
what the product was.

In college, Clay Hunt said:
"It's not what you say,
it's the way that you say it."
It was kind of a chant
the English Department had learned.

If I want to say, for instance,
that I miss the elm trees,
I should tell you:

They held up the sky
over our North Danville farm,
domed and rustling
alive with orioles
soaring on raised arms
perfectly trained to lift
the daily weight of blue.

Or should I just admit:

I can't tell you
how much I miss them.

EARLY IN OUR GARDEN'S CAREER

Another weekend of water;
freshets chortle through our culverts.
Daffodils rest their burdened faces
on the ground. The rain is unrelenting.
We wonder if the land can hold
such insistent giving.

Booted and slickered, we inspect the garden
for disasters. A mole has tunneled
the worn path; water threads
through her browsings in garlic.
The soil releases tiny rivulets
to fill the craters our boots leave.

Lilies nose up, asparagus is purple
as children's fingers in midwinter.
Spring has split the small brain of the pea.
Petals of tulip, thin spatulate hands,
beg their colors from the sun.
Everything is drenched with waiting.

Above our sink, sixty-one tidy quarts
of tomato sauce march across a painting
titled "Parker Products 1943."
They parade right through the column labeled "pints,"
slip under orange matting on the right,
seem to continue well beyond our sight.

Then twenty-six quarts of string beans,
twenty-five of applesauce; blueberries from
burned-over Mount Sunapee.
Raspberry jam in jars of every size and shape,
line up like creatures for the Ark—
awkward with each other, but orderly.

Hours of picking, chopping, cooking down;
filling containers just below the lip, orange
gasket for the seal, the lid clamped down half-tight.
Billows of steam in a sweaty summer kitchen
by the lake. Time pauses for a year or more
in the jars sealed overnight.

It's evening. My mother gets her paper,
brushes, paint. Her legs are swollen.
Seventeen pints of shell beans and corn:
she needs to tally up their beauty.
My father's off trying to win the war.
I am days away from being born.

SOMETHING PERSONAL

Right now, November rain drenches
cold bent grass. A jay accuses,
raucous, tree to tree. It's his habit,
like the custom of a family.
It seems familiar to me,
annoying, reassuring.

I sat with my mother yesterday,
rubbing her hand in our increasingly
companionable silence. I offer an
occasional detail: "Remember
when dad planted eighty pounds of peas?"
for that nibble of response.

I rub her arm, her back,
comb my fingers through her thin hair,
feel her fragile paper skin.
I've relinquished the anger,
but not the ache for conversation
in which both our hearts could speak.

Often when I touch she smiles,
taps her fingers on the pillow
presses my hand against her face
as though she could let go her defense.
As though we could be companions
now nothing is assured.

THE OLD HOME DAY PARADE

Late in the time of dying elms,
down by Rod's Exxon station
where the parade always forms,
next to the yard of the recently abandoned school,
four horses scuff the highway with their iron shoes.

Sixty years ago, right here, the ruts of May
had been worn down into July's dust.
Elwin's hands are full of reins. The horses
are spooked by tractors, the Taylor boy
on his crepe-papered bike, the town band practicing,
eighteen-wheelers grumbling and belching
behind the sheriff's car.

This year's theme is: "East Village: Yesterday and Today,"
same theme as last year and the year before.

Though it never seems they will, enough participants
and watchers show up to make it all worthwhile.
There are, as always, floats
depicting the history of the town.
Committees have been arguing all week
about the way things were
and improvising details all morning.

Up the road, on a scrap of lawn
that hasn't yet slipped down to the river,
next to the pole where Pat Bradley
used to raise the flag each morning,
Ralph Chase Sr. sits in an aluminum folding chair.
The cold of ninety Vermont winters
hides in his afghan-covered knees;
his hands are heavy on his lap.
Helen is in the nursing home this year.

Across the road on the church lawn,
Irene Stanton worries out loud to Anne Smith
that the parade is late again, like always;
she's glad this time she doesn't have to be a judge.
Last year, in order to include everyone,

they invented more categories than were contestants.
Next year she'll sell her home to one of the Ely kids
and pack her things into a single room in town.

The parade begins, crowded into a quarter mile of Route 2
with the ghosts of all the earlier parades
and all that will follow.

The horses first and the rubber-tired wagon,
so there's no one to get hurt if Elwin loses control.
Tart LaBounty follows, grinning at everyone,
squawking the horn of his black Model A,
which doesn't help at all with the horses.
They creep past the bridge where Route 2
used to cross the river to the mill; past the granite blocks
of the mill's foundation guarding the opposite bank;
past the clay pipe, choked with knotweed, through which
a few homes still contribute directly to the river.

The Taylor boy, as usual, can't stay in line,
racing ahead, past Joyce DeWitt and the ladies' kitchen band,
weaving in and out among the Ellis children
(dressed as "the four seasons in East Village")
crepe paper tattering in his wheels. He is overcome
with the present; it is all he can feel;
there is no stopping him.

Ralph's friend Mack Ford who died four years ago,
sits beside him. There are corners of ground
all over town he hayed by hand (scythe and wooden rake)
that now grow up to burdock and willow.

All those places belonged to him; now
they don't belong to anyone.
The barn he stored the summers in
has finally crumbled back into the hillside.

Roland Parenteau, on the old John Deere 50,
who drives equipment up and down this road all summer,
watches the people watching the parade;

he wonders if he will have a stroke the way his father did
and not be able to keep farming.
Maybe in twenty years there'll be a float
about the last farm in the Village.

The church service posed on his hay wagon
doesn't look like any Irene can remember,
but it's good to see the young people,
who quit church so promptly after Sunday school,
make an effort.

The parade has streamed into Parenteau's hayfield
and is reassembling for its return.

Those who have come back for the day walk over to Irene.
Her greeting means their visit is official.
She is the one who does the work of remembering;
she recognizes them at once like the print of an old dress;
Alaska, Ohio, the next town over, they each bring their private past;
they all want to be missed.

The parade returns in some disorder,
like an army attempting a dignified retreat,
dissolves in the schoolyard.

Ralph Jr. and Marge take Ralph Sr.
up to visit Helen at Pine Knoll. They sit together
half an hour without words.

Beside the school the Taylor boy searches through
the sawdust pile in an old tractor tire for pennies
long after the others have given up.
His parents help get chairs and tables
set up for the supper.

Anne Smith drives Irene home across the bridge
to take a nap.

Instead of resting, Irene pokes around the house
she knows she will leave. She stares out

at the plum trees crowding against Ben's woodshed,
which has gone these thirty years without repair,
and at the rotting column of the elm
that used to give them shade.

"Why is it," she wonders,
"the things at hand keep getting smaller
like children's voices from the schoolyard,
and the silence in the house keeps growing?"

LATE WINTER

A season of colors without names,
or none we have patience to use.
Boulders of ice shrugged from highway cliffs,
drained of blue, shrinking in wordless gray;

evergreens gasping in leathered green;
grasses weathered to a dun array.
Even birches are stained by winter's
bite, drained of their radiant white.

What shade the bare branch? Or the limb
shedding bark? The darkness of shriveled
sumac or other browns of loneliness?
The bruised either wait for loveliness

or settle for oblivion—words wither,
are dismissed. Spring never mentions this.

Soft-shell clams have quit the small
tidal flat beside the house; only
a crushed-shell layer of evidence.
Mussels have abandoned every
inch—two hundred-sixteen miles—
of shore the township boasts.

Over crab cakes and roasted
root vegetables we discuss green crabs,
first brought here in ballast water
in the eighteen hundreds, and, like us,
tough, adaptable, not much good
to eat, invading up the coast.

The granddaughter is six weeks old,
still distressed by this assault
of senses. Her mother's milk soothes
only for a moment. Her father
raises oysters to clean the ocean,
capture carbon, make delicious food.

Sunday's paper says this year scallops
perished in Long Island Sound before
they could be caught and eaten; oyster
shells lie empty in the Gulf. We have
no way to keep up with the losses, yet
we all are desperate to comfort her.

PERSPECTIVE

I spend hours pondering
things like electric utilities.
But on the beach am overcome
by the need to wrestle bright snarls
of plastic rope from rows
of drying seaweed.

I've run for office, but in public
embarrass my wife, clutching empty bottles,
coffee cups, cigarette butts,
urgent for a receptacle
to receive them. You know
what it's like.

I offer wizened seed potatoes
to lure my fellow workers to the soil.
I pull stained compostables
from a destiny as trash—it's always
just beyond the boundary
of acceptable.

Whatever this affliction is,
I think I've come to terms with it.
In fact, it feels like freedom.
You smile, but in a few years
you may steal a shopping cart
and join me.

CHAMOIS SHIRT

For decades, I've had a shirt
(actually, a series of shirts)
the color of late-summer wheat,
like our neighbor's golden retriever
(actually, a series of retrievers).
Each swiftly moves from dignified
to comfortable, and rarely
goes to town.

This Christmas, my daughter gave me
another shirt, which provoked
the problem of infinity—that is,
the time between the full use
of one thing, and the first use
of the next; the old shirt you love,
the other you may someday
feel you own.

I was resolute. The bleach stain,
the expanding tear on the left sleeve,
the seams undoing themselves,
gave excuse. I donned the thick
new shirt, brought scissors to the old
and made small garden plots of cloth
to clean the floor, wash windows, put
polish on.

But infinity is always there
beneath, between us. Dogs
wagging their delight, shirt after
shirt, the wheat we wear, the wheat
that will sustain us. Down on my knees
scrubbing today's soil from the floor,
that cloth I use is soft, so thin,
almost gone.

DISTANCE

My mother cared less
and less as she got older.
She casually brushed food dust
off the plates, put them back
on the shelf. The floor,
a sand of crumbs.

We'd chat across the cherry
coffee table. I'd pick stale nuts
from the blue bowl; sip sweet sherry;
take dishes to the sink;
stay too long, scrubbing at
grey slime.

She'd call: "Don't bother!
Come sit and talk with me."
I'd come back, and we'd repeat
a conversation I thought
we'd completed
when I left.

Distance
was the place I stayed
inside myself,
a kind of accusation.
The house was so full
of her leaving.

SHELLING PEAS

Press blossom end, stuffed like a boat's prow;
zip split back toward the stem.
Sometimes the peas are plumped so tight
you have to pry each out. Sometimes they are small,
lost in a vaulted, nearly vacant shell, exploding
with a pop your mouth might make in tasting—
these are the sweetest of them all.

Bright green compliant rows, snap them free;
muted ping on metal bowl, beat of a dance;
so much readiness just waits there hidden.
If there are peas enough there can never be
too many helpers. All ages; each finds their own
determined style—so wildly inefficient
and productive—like raising children.

When Susan's father lived with us
he helped with peas and thrived in company.
A morning watching mist rise, a little rain,
sun's brief prevail, clouds drift by—called it his big-screen TV.
I'd bring peas, a squeaking handful
for him to shell, give him a bowl. He'd fumble;
"Tell me how you open these darned things again."

If we were lucky, grandchildren there to dig peas free,
eat them raw, chase escapees scampering
across the floor. We craved a fresh glossy mound of green
blessed with melting butter.
                    Death sat quietly at Cy's elbow,
present, always a loner, content to watch and linger,
feel the buzz of conversation, the repetition of instruction;
little to offer, never lifting a finger to help.

TOGETHER AGAIN FOR THE FIRST TIME

Familiar musicians play
bluegrass and country, murder
ballads, rollicking anthems
to an indulgent god—heartache,
passionate promises against
all odds. We are cramped and
delighted at the Whammy Bar.

They laugh at almost-missed
transitions, verses that suddenly
disappear; but flawlessly
step in to the mike or back
to alternate, banjo, guitar
and mandolin. Their heads
together for close harmonies.

Song all around us on the road
from Maple Corner home.
Every time the road dips, peepers
and wood frogs join in perfect riot
after winter and before
the summer quiet. So deeply practiced
that it seems to take no effort.

MOOSE BOG

1.

The blue-headed vireo pokes its thread of song
in and out among balsam buds erupting like
green caterpillars, and the first red maple leaves.

Each hop is unpredictable, but decisive;
its body knows just how to stitch shafts
of sun to recovering winter branches.

We hope a spruce grouse will land on that
rotting log, parade for us in the innocent
glory that can make it easy prey for hunters.

It never learns. Today it doesn't come to our
benign impatience; a black-backed woodpecker
hammers and pries its way along a tilting spruce.

2.

We stopped in Island Pond for coffee, talked
with the tired waitress, walked down gravel flecked
with colored plastic, graded to the water.

A loon patrolled, alert, aloof, chick nestled
on its regal back—another summer-only visitor—
unfazed by cottages along the shore.

This is where my father started preaching
sixty years ago. He was laboring
to find his voice and—as he could—to listen.

The once thriving village was collapsing
like a pumpkin in November. The forests
all cut down, the Abenaki and the loggers gone.

The trains still ran, but less often; more
and more of them just passed through.
Stores, churches greyed out of their prosperity.

3.

Today a band of Christians in plain dress,
private, with a message that demands
belief, runs most businesses in town.

They have the energy that drove ambitious
pioneers. Old-timers here can't yet decide
if that's hope or simply too much pride.

At the rail yard western lumber, wrapped
in plastic, waits transfer to become
construction in some optimistic place.

The forest recovers like a ravaged nation,
no pulp mills left to use this spruce and fir.
Some think, "backwater." Some, "salvation."

4.

In the bog, pitcher plants sprout blood-red
blossoms. Sundew closes on its insects,
lip-fingers clasped as though in prayer.

In a beaver pond, dead trees stand sentinel.
A pair of woodpeckers take turns
disappearing in the farthest stem.

No creature here is prospering or seeking
righteousness; just doing what they can
the way they learned since the last glacier.

White admirals are feeding in the puddles
on the road, some broken, one wing
to the ground as pickups pass. Gray jays

hoarding, raucous; moose chomp lily pads;
lynx come back for hares; and we
come hungry from our ordinary lives.

ACCEPTANCE

I don't want to leave those tidy unclean
fictions when I go, like legacies

of a departing colonist. I want loved ones
to find no unused wads of kindness

in my pockets. The wild explosion of
undone will barely notice when I leave—

a garden tilled for fall, cover crop of rye,
subversive common seeds I might consider

weeds buried there in wait. The nephew
I hardly ever hear from, hardly ever call,

who wore the uniform in both Korea
and Iraq, makes a living fixing

roofs, floors, patios—you name it—there in
Texas; bass-fishes after work and weekends.

I keep pretending silence is respect.
Why don't I talk with him about his mother?

Why did the dahlias never bloom this year,
when they were in full fervor last? I realize

my first garden shed may never get the fix
I planned this season. My grandson might

keep shrugging when I reach to touch him
and I, keep aching for a reason.

"Misery loves company," I sometimes tell
myself, as though it might be comfort;

but really? I never find new friends there.
My misery's an excuse, tailored to postpone

my fingers from the dirt—the fear I need to touch—
its truth there, waiting patient as a stone.

PREACHER VISITS

1.

They bother the neighbors, yards like his,
with damaged cars of dubious ambition;
hope rusting another year on blocks
like a waiting replacement transmission.

Assembled—as though they might be useful—
thick fluids darkening the ground:
clutches disengaged, strips of chrome, wheel rims,
all promised new life, still lying around.

My friend talked car improvement till my mind
stuck in neutral. December visits I'd leave
with my annual request: that he come sing
solo, "O, Holy Night" on Christmas Eve.

2.

In the village, a house where knotweed crowds
front steps; trees link branches across windows;
clapboards (white paint flaking) curl, slip,
protect less every year from winter's snows.

I knew the couple who lived there long ago.
Her African violets on every downstairs shelf;
he kept the fire going long as he could;
she tried; couldn't manage by herself.

Both gone. I don't know if the children
disagreed, or—swamped by their own lives—didn't care.
No one mows or plows. The apple tree blossoms
in spring. Summer, wild roses grace the air.

3.

Unlike improvement, dissolution
doesn't rush or rest; it doesn't find
our judgment relevant. Call it indifferent,
but there's no test to pass; it's not unkind.

In the kitchen where floor sagged toward
rotting sill, violets thrived, faucet squealed;
the coffee was delicious. I was learning—
just companionship, nothing to be healed.

And my friend with grease-dark fingers
and no inclination toward belief, sang
with untethered beauty at the service. But
plans for the Camaro gave him more relief.

CHURCH ON THE COMMON

It is too large now, far too large
for the village. No conviction
to be summoned, no congregation
equal to its ambition.

The vaulted sanctuary
assumes an antique holiness.
Hymnals warp slowly. An ermine
is quite efficient with the mice.

The faithful, as they are called,
keep to the works of maintenance.
The rest of us tolerate their grumble,
preserve a safe ambivalence.

But, for the ghost-white owl, paused
by the stilled bell, we assemble.
It wants its way. Its presence fills
the silence. We watch and tremble.

DESCENT

Mother's parents wisped like shadows through our lives;
they'd sent her off to school in Canada. Grandfather—
someone I read about but never talked to.
Our grandmother, a bitter recluse—I never
heard her voice. A painting of hers sits in the corner—
a bleak winter day, tortured branches bending.

       An attic of discontinued conversations
       is what's left of our inheritance. Early
       ancestors "knew what things were worth."
       Coal, tin, copper, railroads—appropriating
       value from their workers and the earth—
       which their children promptly started spending.

They got better at it every generation:
stately homes, fine prints, genteel collections,
bookbinding, poetry that rarely touched the ground.
Then, the lovely things themselves sold off.
Now much of the legacy we've found
is boxed-up accounts of finances descending.

       Not like the missionaries on my father's side—
       no yearning to pass through the needle's eye.
       Though one aunt sold china and some rare cut glass
       to help my parents buy their Vermont farm,
       and settle back into the working class
       (still with a flair for upper-class pretending.)

We seem executors of a reduced estate.
                    But then
my cousin visits; we sort through photos,
letters; toss things out, eat, laugh.
               And with a brother,
twenty years of silence breaks into conversation.
Blow off the dust and accumulated fears
that kept fractures from a healthy mending.

       They had a steam launch and a summer
       residence up in the Thousand Islands.
       We might go as tourists, see the family name

on some small street. We find pictures of crowds
watching the great hotel engulfed in flame;
fascinated by an impressive ending.

The school basement was a concrete box
we played in when the weather forced us.
We gave concerts there, singing "songs of many nations"
and anthems for each branch of the military,
with parents lined up at the metal rail above.

For basketball, a red stripe across the middle;
foul lines came almost to that center.
Hoops at each end, three feet from the ceiling
(which was the floor of Mrs. Sleeper's first four grades.)
We all shot flat and hard.

The girls could only run three steps,
then had to pass and could not cross
the center line—but played just like the boys at recess.

The walls were out-of-bounds; the ball was put in play
one foot on cement. When teams from Danville, Barnet, or Monroe
were Visitors, they found momentum was their enemy.
We turned neatly, like a tractor raking to the fence;
they hit the wall; we got the ball.

We never lost a game at home.
The Lynaughs, Langmaids, Gadapees
passed and dribbled through the forests
of those neighbor teams.

Amazingly we won in their gyms too,
exploding on those spacious maple floors,
still passing, dribbling, and shooting flat,
our families huddled in the stands.

Upstairs: the learning.
Each row was a grade; we always knew
the lessons for the next year.
Ronnie Amidon, who lent me his small horse
to ride the mile up to our farm
and back again each morning for the bus
kept trying to get right the lessons of last year.

The teacher tapped out her annoyance on his shoulder,
looked over at me, smiled, almost confidentially,
shrugged as if to say, "What can you do?"
as though this was the lesson he had come for.

OUR TURN

I'm startled by the comfort it gives me
to cook and clean the house—blueberry
pancakes for each guest, scrubbed counters
that say, "Thank you, I can rest now,"

as I go off to do the same. My father acted
as though righteousness woke every morning
with no need to wash its face. How easily,
he implied, the vacuum or a casserole

might distract him from the search for truth.
I've learned to trust a pot of coffee and another
sweep of wood stove litter. I delight in
grandchildren who bring untidiness and joy.

I'm learning, as my mother sometimes did,
to love from the distance of a dishpan, listen
to every note, alert for the shift or word
that will sustain the lilt of conversation.

I miss them both now. I want my father
to come back and help me put away
the dishes. I'd hug my mother who left
still clutching her childhood like a strange coin.

But this is our house to rebuild, and they, the guests.
I'd invite their patience to conversations
that were never welcomed. Grandchildren will bring
the emptied plates, help us set the table.

AFFECTION

The forecaster says, "This time
I really mean it, frost everywhere,
not just in colder valleys."
And the weather seems to mean it
too. The clear day has that steel
glint in its smile. Three remaining
gladiolas, barely pink and yellow;
five sunflowers sprouting
from a fallen stalk; I rescue
them for last bouquets.

The dahlias insist they can bloom
like this forever: "We're just getting
started; see the buds on every stem?"
I would never argue with them.
I just ask if they would like
to come inside and be adored.
"Well, since you put it that way..."
they consent. "And make sure you bring
along those foolish bees who cling
with such insistence to our faces.
They act as though we were
the only flowers left on earth."

NATURE PEE
(as my grandson calls it)

Bright green patches
grow lush and taller
than surrounding lawn.
They look to me
like gratitude.

They remind me of pasture
grass cropped down, but
dotted with patches of vibrant
green, among thistles
and slowly drying cow flops.

Sometimes pasture was the only place
we could find for playing catch;
though, of course, it had its perils.
Grounders were dangerous.
"Clean catch" had a special meaning.

The lawn declares that I've
made many trips out here.
Sometimes I even visit
in the winter. No neighbors
in sight, and it's sustainable.

I tell myself and all my grandsons
I don't want this place
mistaken for the suburbs.
As I look around I think:
"At least I got that done."

FOR MY UNCLE

We are picking raspberries
in the bramble tangle
that your carefully tended bed has become.

After all those years giving,
this was the place for savoring,
this home you called "summer"
staying from spring to fall.

You could not come this summer or the last.
We phoned to ask permission;
your frail voice cheerful with consent.

The thunderstorm gathers, eager,
but strangely indecisive.

We pick with familiar greed—
sometimes pluck from the litter of fallen purpled fruit
or pinch pink almost-ripe till they release,
knowing we won't get back in time.

We lift arches to find berry clans,
pick so many at once they stain our hands;
turn back down the same path
for the clever, furtive ones.

Strangers have already been here, trampled vines.
Two ash trees, a few burdock, have moved in.
Even the bear may come.

The rain releases just as we are done.

All the time we picked
you were there with us, welcoming, "yes"
to this place you are leaving
with that other "yes."

MY OBITUARY

I've decided to get it over with
and write my own obituary.

Others have done it
with a lilt of self-awareness—
saying things loved ones
might have thought but not dared say—
at least not in the paper.

I'll take it one step further, publish it now
before the ink is dry on my own life.
I'd hate to miss those comments
that get muttered over breakfast
falling crumb-like from the table.

I might even create an online account,
solicit feedback, both about my life so far
and the integrity of the obit.

Why wait for them to shovel
the unsaid over my casket,
six feet of conclusions,
tamped down as grief?

What stays unsaid is sharp as broken glass,
or damp and moldy from the silence,
sometimes locked in closets, because
who knows what damage it might do
beyond what it's already done?

I'd prefer a living document—
updates on any changes;
forgivenesses I've sought; new friendships gained;
even hopes—my own and others—damaged irreparably, but
no longer draped in silence.

Consider this an outline
of a new undertaking—
a form of early truth release—
a chance to let that puppy courage off the leash.

If you do not come to know yourselves
then you exist in poverty.
                    –Gospel of St. Thomas

That sudden clench
of jaw
            your body
                        feels it

grind fine powder
from your teeth

the hand that squeezes
till it hurts
                        someone

the foot that
                shoves the cat
too hard
            against the wall

the cat knows
the children know

this is revelation
                        staring at you
right now
                trying
                        generous

valiant as a mirror

your own eye
                stutters
darts
        away

but   there it is

something
            you can't ever
                            again
dismiss as ordinary

SALVAGING BEAUTY

(for Alan)

Peonies are blooming
        to the point of collapse.
                They lean into each other
                        with nothing to say.
                        Gracing lawn and stones,
                thousands of fragrant petals,
        extravagant as wings
relinquished.

To make final bouquets, I take
        every flower that does not dissolve
                at touch—late blooms, buds
                        surrounding first display—
                        pinks, bold and blushed;
                shameless yellow;
        white, center-stained
with crimson.

Every vase chipped
        or cracked I fill;
                        vases on every table in the house.
                        I leave the lawn
                scattered
        with petals and stems.
        I wait for the gathered scents
to overcome me.

COMING AND GOING

Late Tuesday evening I return
the rented car to Enterprise.
Another trip to advocate for less
completed. Increasingly,
on my pauses here, I've looked
across the river. Frayed blue
tarpaulins are draped between
poplars; an encampment
among the concrete footings
of some abandoned industry.

On this side, commerce still
acts as though it is inevitable.
But tonight the thrushes are
speaking. The breathy flute
of a veery, and, deeper
in recovering forest,
an imperfect echo from a hermit
reminds that yesterday
is ancient. We could lose them;
we could lose tomorrow.

I listen, and a wisp of human
conversation I cannot decipher
comes to me from the tents
across the river. Just a thin
summer trickle and the leaves
between us. I may never
understand. I hear the engine
ticking as it slowly loses
confidence. I wait for my wife
to come and take me home.

RECOGNITION

He stands by the rock wall and roses,
stares across the valley at Northfield hills.
Sometimes, it seems, he just comes to cry.

Our driveway, house, lawn where he waits,
are on land clawed and leveled from rough
pasture that sloped uphill from his home.

Our garden, snug inside its fence, was
his back yard. There are visits from many
who once lived here, tugged like ghosts.

Some stay and wait for recognition.
I go out to stand with him. "I know the house
is gone, but I don't have any other place."

A hummingbird thrums past, lands
for sugared water on the red plastic feeder.
"What was that?" he calls out, astonished.

"You must have seen them when you lived here."
"Oh no, they hadn't come up with them yet,"
he says. We watch it drink and dart away.

I know what he means. Each year it feels
my eyes create the chestnut-sided warbler
singing all over this garden when I first

put its tiny body and its slender song
together. And every June the grief
of apple blossoms stuns me with departure.

I say, "Wait," go inside, find the chipped
white aggies streaked with blue the soil
keeps offering, return them to their owner.

Early spring in their new house—he'll show me
everything. Here's the abandoned fort,
a roof of lashed sticks, tan woven plastic,
covering a gap between two boulders.
Twigs collect on top. Leaves on the floor
are almost dry; stone seats suggest
a welcome. He stays outside. It's not
quite fear that heeds the privacy
someone created, then abandoned here.

    Orange plastic tied on yellow birch;
    he explains this means the land that's theirs
    ends here; the space beyond is somehow
    different, maybe dangerous. And yet
    the ground is little changed from one step
    to the next—last bits of snow, mossy
    stones, brown leaves hugging sapling
    roots, white birch porched with fungus
    have claimed both sides equally their own.

It takes almost no encouragement
to cross the hesitation in his mind.
We explore along the ridge until
we find the back side of a neighbor's lawn
and house—as deer must on their rounds.
Small boats on racks, two mold-stained sheds,
a desultory fence, sketch the line
between another human residence
and a more cautious, watching presence.

    To our right: a small ledge, or what
    he calls a cliff; but here the rock is gone
    and there's a steep but safe way down.
    His small determined yellow boots follow
    his exploring mind. I realize
    this was his destination all along:
    tall pines, a bowl of wildness that right now
    belongs to him, a distant cliff, rocks,
    puddles filmed with ice, soon to be gone.

His body quickens with adventure.
He stomps into pools that flood his feet.
I suggest the names for trees, birdsongs;
he collects, as I relinquish them.
Beside the pine, he likes "midden"
as we marvel at brown hulls stripped
from pitch-stained skeletons of cone.
"Why did they pull them all apart?"
"Seeds hidden at the base of every one."

      Puddle to puddle, snow and turkey track;
      we have come to the cliff's other side.
      Grey slabs in slow motion creep down the ledge,
      jumbled—black caves, fern-laced at each edge,
      almost a stairway back. I tell him
      I could lift him to that level place
      and we could climb up over. He shakes
      his head, smiles, "Sorry grandpa, I might
      next time, right now I'm just scared."

We take the long way home. Pebbled with
deer-drops, the path skirts another house.
A slab and pole that held a TV dish
are rusting quietly. He wants to be
a deer, watch here from behind the trees
next to the driveway—close, observing,
unseen. He won't step out on the lawn.
We climb to the dirt road, then wander home
through stubbled fields just commencing green.

SUMMER RUN

For Sadie
       a bird is an explosion
           in the brain.

My words bounced
       like butterflies off a rhinoceros
           that day by the river
                when the sandpiper led her up and down

a half mile of meadow
       piping, keening, dipping,
           feigning peril in her flight
               skimming the mown grass.

I stood there
       red leash trailing on the ground

trying to figure
       who was doing what to whom

while my dappled dog
       raced in the wind.

Oh! The urge to call her back—

but this was neither love nor war
           and everything was fair

and each did everything she could
           to help the other fly.

THE UNRULINESS OF BROCCOLI

It seems well-mannered in the store,
clumped by orange rubber bands
or twisted wire, sometimes three or four
heads bunched in an intensive seminar.

In trays, sliced, with celery and carrots,
it waits to be finger food. Frozen in
dismembered chunks for microwave or pot,
it seems resigned to being good.

But in the garden broccoli wants it all;
"Can't you see I need more compost here!"
It mushrooms to a basketball.
My knife can barely find the stalk.
Side shoots wait for the big head to fall.

Succulent caterpillars in team colors
lurk in the inner forest chewing to create
the next rhapsody of butterflies,
but cooked…curled protein on the plate.

Late summer; I have picked and picked,
and picked again. The shoots take over,
dark green, plump, surging into flower,
yellow, functional, triumphant in their hour.

FEED THE CATS

Upon my waking, the cats'
first and urgent task is to
remind me—before bathroom,
before toothbrush—that
nothing is more important
than feeding them.

      Some communities believe
      their supplication drags
      the laggard sun up
      morning's sky. Never
      would it rise (or the can
      be opened) but for them.

The sun has its practiced
ways of coping. I am inclined
to groggy banter, which
is stolidly ignored.
Pat-pat down the stairs—
my only choice, to follow.

      When I am home all day
      the cats are at my feet,
      insisting on the evening
      feeding at 1:00. It rouses
      them from the daily round
      of dedicated relaxation.

I wonder, when I give up
and feed them at 3:00
whether there's a sense
of triumph.
      I've seen nothing
that could be considered
excessive celebration.

GREY GLACIER
(Patagonia)

Downriver
from the ancient
shrinking field
of winter stone,
grey rocks
smaller than
clenched fists
are heaped
like evidence.

They chink, grate,
yield at my
unsteady step.
Colors dissolve
in this expanse
of patience;
grey water,
grey sky.
The electric muted
blue of icebergs
the only thing
that tugs the eye.

The water
clouds itself,
licks powder
from the stones,
piles them up
won't
leave them alone.

Flat disc
in my
crooked finger
at water's edge,
I bend low,
skip it upstream
toward the laden snow.

RELINQUISHED

Back of the drawer, back of the closet,
back forty, back of the mind. The knife

that once sliced everything you ate—
years untouched. Toothbrush that your mouth

forgot. The stiff glove your grandson
discovers, claims as perfect for a catch.

Shirts, dusty colors growing older,
fading together shoulder to shoulder.

Briefcases; canvas, leather, vinyl;
stuffed with such important papers once.

Up on the hill, a cutter bar bares
its teeth to the wind. Stone wall, dump rake

sprouting cherry and poplar. Timothy
crowded by goldenrod, thistles,

invading ash. Tall fronds gone to seed;
a swarm of goldfinch drops to feed.

Faces, intimacies, ideas, the food
that stirred your breath and fed your blood;

even dread that woke you fevered.
Ham and beets, potatoes, carrots, fried

in such savory red-flannel hash.
Tuna casseroles you no longer share

with families you were sure you knew
in villages you now rarely drive through.

Silences accumulate; stay there
without drama or decision. Changed

without changing, cracked paint, windows
dry-eyed and un-grieving. So hard

to admit—yet you must admit—you call
this home, but you are always leaving.

LEEKS

The leaves become their
stockings underground.
By fall the stems are layers
of thin socks tugged up on
each other—no feet at all.

I plant early, deep;
slim threads with catfish
mouths for roots. Green
stretching up, white
knitting itself south.

So little drama:
no flowers or raucous vines.
I mound handfuls
of soil to hide stalks
deeper in the ground.

I loosen with a fork,
coax the long stem up;
strip outer leaf down
to a black fist of soil—
expose the pearly sheaf.

Stacked in my basket,
like a wagon of small
lumbered trees—I will
have thick soup before
December's iron freeze.

BARN SWALLOW

It was always dusk in the barn—light
from gaps between boards aging gray
and a small house-shaped opening
inviting swallows.

A week after I got the BB gun
I stood in the barn, watching shiny
copper pellets arc toward
copper-breasted birds,
perched there as though waiting.
It felt like curiosity, not malice.

Then, blue feathers fluttered from the rafter.
I stared at my weapon. I lifted the bird,
amazed at its sudden emptiness,
unable to find the place death entered.

HOME FROM HIDALGO

Not the priest who declared independence
for Mexico, or the state named in his honor,
but the restaurant on State Street, Media, PA.
The owner, Queen of her daughters
and the patrons they serve. Accompanied
by sudden music, she breaks into songs
of loss and sadness when the food is late,
till we all start clapping, singing, and forget.

Two hours later, when the Hidalgo chicken
is finished and late October rain begins
Gabriel asks: "Can I ride home on your shoulders?"
He has grown two inches; I have lost a half;
we won't be doing this for long, so, "of course."
He points with his fingers to steer through the
darkness of Jackson Street; I stagger from one edge
of the sidewalk to another as he knew I would.

The rain intensifies. It becomes a sudden
race. "Accelerate! Accelerate!" Gabriel cries.
I tell him I am turning on the afterburners
which is, of course, another Abuelo fart joke.
We stumble home before the torrent.
                                        I am
delighted Mexico got free; that the Queen has come to
Media; that my grandchildren speak Spanish.
That we get to carry them once more up Jackson Street.

HUMILITY

It took twenty-five years for rot
to test my choice to work the land
inside this fence. Slowly, I forgot

those days of labor; mind and hands;
selecting a correct position;
setting posts, wire, gates. The plan

to change the hillside's wild condition
seemed wise, but had the arrogance
of easy ownership ambition.

Not rot alone, but a cruel chance
laid the gate twisted on stone stairs—
a scold to my entitled permanence.

Deer came late winter. Cold stars,
a gate left open (no crop to grow);
perhaps a dog bark; the sudden fear

made this a wire prison. The doe
hurled herself against the fierce surprise
of fence again and yet again. The slow

harsh breath, the failed attempt to rise,
the crooked angles of leg and head,
wild realization in her eyes.

And all the confidence and pride—
delight in the good things I raise
and share with friends eager to be fed—

melted like spring snow. These April days,
a time to reconsider. Should I
rebuild a gate that tries to say

who may and who may not drop by
for sustenance? A strange distress,
almost a confession. That panicked eye

is skin torn from my cleverness.
Our good food feels like an illusion—
the loss has soured our success.

But still, I reach the gardener's conclusion
that of course we must have carrots, beans,
corn, arugula in fall profusion.

Rebuilding the gate now means
I get another, chastised chance
to waltz with many shades of green,

a few more years, a final dance;
a gift more measured, understood—
not an assertion of endurance.

I built it back, brought cedar wood,
pried out the stumps, dug the holes again,
stapled back the wire. I thought I could

not do it, but I did; even wore pain
from my effort like a silent boast,
too satisfied, too proud to complain.

When I have joined the league of ghosts
will the soil's next guests have learned the art
of knowing they are visitors, not hosts?

The land keeps saying "Stop! If you must start,
remember you are here by gift. Begin
with the instruction of a broken heart."

COMPANIONSHIP

A friend gave us these tomatillos, husked
and sticky; another brought tomatoes, yellow,
sweet. November third, I can't believe it!
I added our own garlic and cilantro,
oregano from right outside the door,
onions, peppers, hanging out
in the refrigerator. I threw in ocean salt
and cumin from an undetermined place.
Lime, I admit, from somewhere south.
A dash of syrup from some nearby trees.

If I hadn't made this salsa now, the key
ingredients (which wait for no one) would
have perished with the season, squandering
themselves without a second thought.
Instead, friends surround the island
in the kitchen. Before bowl and chips
make it to the table, what was the conversation
topic becomes, itself, the conversation.
We scoop, exclaim, laugh, mouths
full of ingredients, improvisation.

GRATITUDE

The peonies and gladiolas are more
seductive every fall. I choose slips

of peony root with three buds full
of color that may prosper years from now.

I dig shaggy gladiola corms,
plumped on slender stalks, next year's

replacements for the tough exhausted husks
left from the thrust of color-trumpets to the sky:

purple (steeped in black), regal crimson,
slim white Abyssinian, lavender

that cried out to sunset orange;
bulblets cling, intent on futures of their own:

Beauty's nonchalant kindness
accepts the slow learning of my eyes.

A few days of October sun—they seem
like gratitude, always a surprise.

I plant the slips; come in and sort the corms;
possessed by past and future blooms.

I remember how I dreaded
grownups who creaked like closing doors.

Even now I fear joy might never
be allowed back through my window,

but gratitude's a different eye that opens—
unnerving in its great permissions.

In sun, on this cold porch, I'm grateful.
Some shy part of me is always

sitting here, no wisdom, no plan; full
of psalms, no notion who I'm singing to.

LAKE ELMORE, OCTOBER FIRST

1.

Curled beige feathers, downy at the base,
litter the stream that wanders toward us
and Elmore's lake. Beavered alder branches,

submerged pond-hair cushions, duckweed
corralled by viburnum roots, all strewn
as though by a gentle pillow fight.

We paddle past managed shorelines with tidy
cottages, to this neighborhood of lily pads
and pickerel weed, hidden from their sight.

More happens here, like the basement daycare
center, chorused with children, always cluttered,
doing a better business than the church.

This is the water's sweet meander, slow
channel where merganser, mallard grew.
It's also where the storm flood races through.

2.

My grandson cried when he gave up
his first and favorite bike, the one he trusted
enough to let his feet release the ground.

I had to argue with myself against
the urge to dry his eyes, hurry him along;
stop, honor that lonely keening sound.

Two young ducks try to keep one bend upstream
from us. Trapped by our invasion, they finally
stop. One leaps to flight, the other hides

behind marsh grass in a small alder pocket.
We paddle by, eyes averted, our
small courtesy. It quivers as we pass.

Six summer weeks this was their home;
now they leave for something new.
I think: "detachment—that's illusion too."

3.

In the next pool a heron rises—scarecrow
taking flight. We look for it at each next
bend, plying its silent heron tricks again.

But a beaver pond opens before us,
flood at eye level. No heron, but wide water
seeping through a thousand sticks.

This summer we went up five streams.
The beaver—dogged Calvinists—seem to insist
it's effort, not the dam, that's permanent.

We postpone leaving, poke up every bulrush
alley, give in at last; turn, stroke hard across
the open reach, land on the expanse of beach.

Women in bright saris watch their boisterous
men play tag, joined by the youngest daughter.
We greet them, lift the boat, leave our visit in the water.

LATE AUTUMN DAY

Warm and lazy as June
though the sun will set at 4:15.
The promised snow
has time to bring its joy
by morning. Jays and
chickadees flit in for seed
from pine and elm. Fruit flies
cluster on pears and wine.

We sit on the porch sorting
through Christmas ornaments
my parents will not touch
again. What would each
child or grandchild choose
to take back to their tree?
The wooden cat? Crocheted
angel stuffed with cotton?

Perhaps the mouse in a
walnut shell? Something
they made, in a time
of simple gifts.
We sit in autumn sun
as the storm comes on,
and weather, grief, and love
proceed unsupervised.

NOTES

About the cover art: the painting was done for a series called *The Cycle of Animals,* with this piece representing Libra, for balance, in the Zodiac. From the artist: "This painting addresses the precarious nature of Bicknell's Thrush, which is among the land bird species of highest conservation concern in North America. It's breeding habit is geographically restricted fir-dominated forests in the northeastern U.S. and southeastern Canada. It is highly sensitive to deforestation."

p. 7: "Mississippi Kites" Some Texas towns have anti "weedy lot" ordinances which would have prevented the Audubon Sanctuary in Frontera. A special wildlife habitat ordinance was passed to make it possible (fronteraaudubon.org/2016/04/04/thicketearlydays).

p. 17: My brother died from a ruptured brain aneurysm.

p. 54: "Wild Turkeys" This poem was written in the early 1980s, when wild turkeys had not yet reached Vermont's Northeast Kingdom, and we wondered if they could survive there. Not wondering about that now!

THANKS

Susan Sussman, my wife, has been a tireless and patient companion in my writing efforts. She knows what she likes and what she doesn't. That helps. But she has also become an increasingly tough and insightful critic, learning to specify what works and doesn't for her. I have come to trust her reactions—and accept her affection even when a particular poem may not occasion enthusiasm.

My brothers Steve Parker, and Malcolm (Mac) Parker have been offering support and smart feedback for years. Often, I have reached Steve by cell phone with an insistent reading of a first draft while he pauses from work in a Christmas tree field. Mac offers steady insight, understanding and encouragement. He also helps me understand the importance of presentation.

Thanks to: Sara Forward for her insightful feedback and for being the editor who set me on the path to publication; Ann Aspell for her friendship, support, critique and strategic advice; my sisters-in-law Linda Sussman and Emily-Sue Sloane for their important reactions and comments.

Judith Chalmer encouraged me to discover the joys of re-writing. Thanks to Marjorie Ryerson, Samn Stockwell, and Carol Henrickson for their ongoing feedback, companionship, and help shaping a number of these poems in our poetry group. And to Samantha Kolber for her effective review of both individual poems and the volume as a whole (several times!). She offered the first really comprehensive feedback on much of my writing.

Gratitude to Wyn Cooper for his professional and immensely helpful review of the details, the poems, and of the volume as a whole. Sometimes line-by-line edits, sometimes chop and slash, but mostly showing what he thought worked well, what didn't work at all, and what might be made better. He kept pointing toward the kind of poetry I should be trying for.

Finally, thanks to my daughters Katie and Emily for their patience, forgiveness and love.

SCUDDER H. PARKER grew up on a family farm in North Danville, Vermont. He's been a Protestant minister, state senator, utility regulator, candidate for Governor, consultant on energy efficiency and renewable energy, and is settling into his ongoing work as a poet. He's a passionate gardener and proud grandfather of four. He and his wife, Susan, live in Middlesex, Vermont.